Jutta Lammèr

Fun with Felt

Watson-Guptill Publications

New York

Contents

Introduction

The Material

Felt is a particularly attractive material, out of which one can make both simple and quite complicated objects. Hardly any other fabric of this quality offers such a wide range of beautiful, pure colours, or proves so easy and neat to work with.

Above all, working in felt represents an important stage on the way to domestic needlework—from the childish scissors and paper to the sewing-machine and household materials for clothes, underwear and curtains. Felt can be cut like paper and used like a woven fabric, while the tedious job of binding and over-stitching cut edges is obviated. The beginner can practice neatness in cutting out and the intelligent assembly of different pieces of material, and so acquire the basic principles of dressmaking, without going through a lot of boring exercises.

Felt isn't a cheap material, but it has great advantages. It doesn't tear, it's extraordinarily hard-wearing, and it's washable. It can be ironed and, of course, cleaned. With a few exceptions, felt is made of pure wool, pressed instead of woven. It has no wrong side, and is sold in double width; but if you only need a little you can get a cutting out of a half-width.

There are three standard qualities: curtain felt, garment felt and decorative felt. The objects shown in this book were chiefly made of garment felt. Curtain felt, sold only in a few dark colours, is not suitable for hobby work, but decorative felt is always used as covering or coating material.

Felt is sold in drapery stores, fabric departments of most department stores and hobby shops, though in the latter mostly in rather small pieces, and consequently at a higher price. If you are using felt for a hobby it is more economical to buy it by the yard at a drapery store. The price of garment felt in double width depends on colour and quality. Decorative felt is a good deal cheaper.

Equipment

No special equipment is needed. Felt is cut with sharp, medium-sized scissors and sewn with ordinary needles or by machine. For gluing it, use a gelatinous adhesive that won't make spots on the material. (*Don't* use an all-purpose glue!). The cutting-out pattern can be drawn with a soft pencil, straight on the wrong side of the felt, the lines being rubbed out later. Apart from scissors, adhesive and a soft pencil, you should have some plastic sheet handy, for trying out the composition of the pieces, especially those intended for appliqué work.

Composition

The wide choice of colours available in felt may lead one to attempt combinations that prove only momentarily attractive, to it is wise to observe this fundamental rule: the more striking the contrast between the colours chosen, the more discreet one must be in their decorative use, whether as appliqué motifs, ties or borders, or in interwoven effects. For instance, if you are planning the work in pink and violet—which can be very attractive—you must confine yourself to these two colours, keeping one of them well in the foreground. With equally strong colours one should always let one predominate and reserve the other as a subordinate contrast. If you don't keep to this rule of thumb your work will appear restless and inharmonious. It is another matter if you want to combine a number of equally brilliant colours in a figured design. In that case, of course, you can put a lot of colours alongside of one another, taking care, however, to keep the background of this kind of appliqué work neutral—i.e. in a subdued colour. When choosing designs to be applied to cushions, folders, paper-cases and so forth, the same moderation is called for. Felt is a lively material in itself, and is spoilt by flourishes and fantasies. It ought not even to be combined with materials of another texture, such as raffia, silk, or synthetic weaves. On the other hand, work done in wool-yarn upon it—embroidery or crochet—can look very well, because felt itself is made of wool.

The models shown in this book are only intended to stimulate your creative skill and help you to gain experience through simple work, finding your way, step by step, to professional expertise.

Glued work

Book jacket

Materials:

1 piece of dark-green felt, 20 inches $\times$ height of book

1 piece of light-green felt the same size.

The dimensions depend on the size of the book when closed. Measure this horizontally over the front cover, the spine and the back cover, and allow another $2\frac{1}{2}$ inches on both sides for the turn-ins. Then draw a line with a pencil across the piece of dark felt from side to side, $\frac{1}{2}$ inch inside the top and bottom edges, and mark off $2\frac{1}{2}$ inches from the upright edges. The space inside these four lines must then be divided by vertical lines $1\frac{1}{4}$ inches apart, beginning from the outer end of the front cover, stopping at the spine, and then marking the back cover in the same way. The distance between the lines next to the spine will differ according to the width of the spine. Sometimes it will work out exactly right, but this need not be so. Of course the distance between the vertical lines could be specially calculated, but this would prove too difficult for beginners. After marking the lines, cut them in a single movement with sharp scissors. Instead of inserting the points of the scissors to begin with, start the line carefully with either a pen-knife or a razor blade, and then go ahead with the scissors.

Next, cut long widthways strips from the light felt, which, when the book is closed, will reach from the outer edge of the front cover to that of the back cover, plus $2\frac{1}{2}$ inches the turn-ins. Reckon the width of the strips

Book-jacket and book-marker
made of interwoven strips of felt.
A job that older children can
easily carry out

by the height of the book, minus the borders you marked off from the top and bottom. The cut strips should be as nearly as possible the same width as the spaces between the vertical slits, i.e. $1\frac{3}{4}$ inches. With an ordinary octavo volume you will get seven strips of that width, or as near as may be. Having measured and cut the light-green strips, you must now weave them through the dark ground from right to left, over and under as in darning or paper-weaving: one light strip over, and the next under, the dark one. When you have pulled them all through and evened the ends, glue them down on the front and back turn-ins and press them for a short time under a weight. Those lying on top of the turn-in must reach to the edge of it.

The flap you turn in round the back cover of the book must be left loose, so that the cover can be used for a wider book, but the front cover must have a flap $1\frac{1}{2} \times 2\frac{1}{2}$ inches glued to the inside at the top, and another against the bottom fold, the glued part being about half an inch wide. These flaps are then folded inwards over the top and bottom of the book jacket, and the turn-in is firmly glued to them (see drawing). The turn-ins could, of course, be simply sewn to the cover at the top and bottom of the front side, but this never looks really workmanlike—it's always a bit 'cock-eyed'. Besides which, you would have to allow a little extra height.

If you want to feel absolutely sure that everything is going to hold together, you can glue the strips together where they cross one another but this is not really necessary. It always looks nice if you make a book-marker to match, out of the same

2"
1 3/16"
1 3/16"
1 3/16"
1 3/16"
1 3/16"
1 3/16"
1 3/16"
1 3/16"
1 3/16"
1 3/16"
2"
3/8"

Glue flap on here
Turn in and
glue to flap
Turn flap in like this

Bookjacket with flap
Book cover

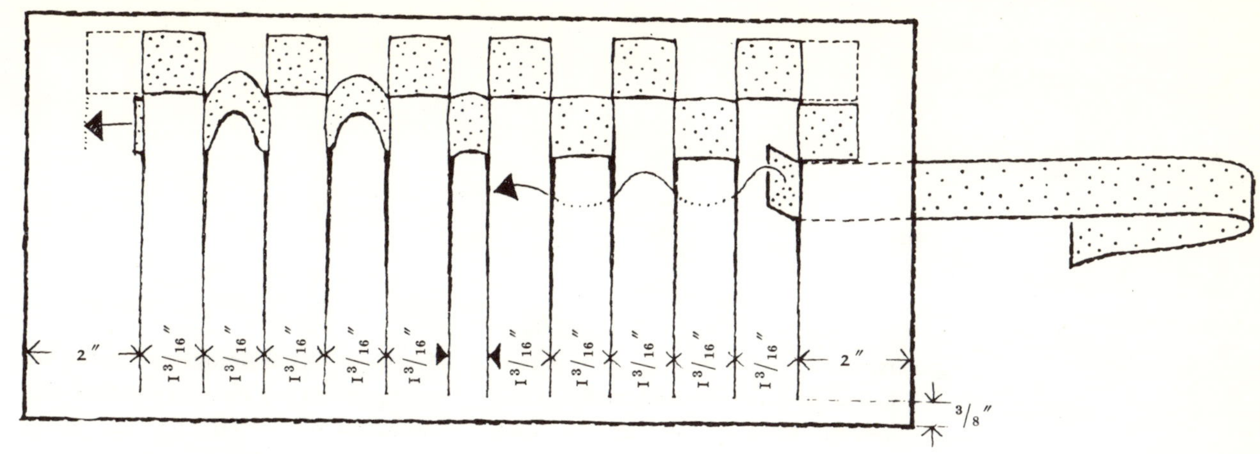

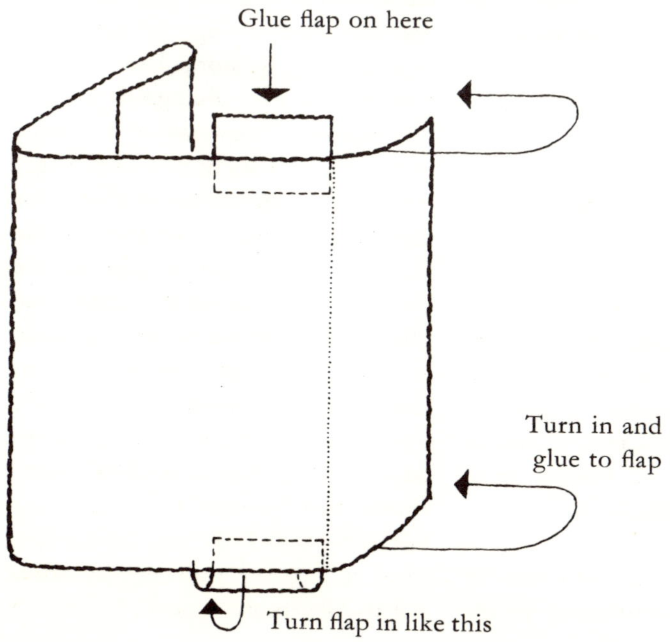

11

material, and with the same pattern. Cut a strip of felt, and make evenly-spaced vertical slits in the lower third of the length. Weave narrow strips of felt in and out of these and fasten the ends with neat stitches, (see front cover).

Writing-table set for a girl

Materials:

1 piece of light-green felt, 40 × 8 inches, or 2 pieces, 20 × 8 inches and the same amount in orange (for the book rests), smaller scraps of felt in orange and green for blotter, pen-tray and writing-pad.

Enamelled metal book rests can be bought in pairs in stationery shops. These will have orange felt glued on them, leaving $\frac{1}{2}$-inch beyond all the edges, to be turned over and glued down. The inside of the rests is covered in light-green felt. The edges are cut after gluing,—if preferred, with pinking scissors. Use a gelatinous adhesive for gluing.

An enamelled pen-tray of a simple shape can be bought at a stationer's. The corners should be rounded for ease in covering. Coat the outside with glue, with special care at the corners and thick edges. Cover the glued surface with a fairly large piece of light-green felt, pressing it on firmly and compressing it or spreading it out till every wrinkle is removed. Let it dry, then trim off the edges neatly with scissors. To make the felt cling under the moulded edge, press it into the groove with some not too sharp instrument.

The pen-tray is lined in the same way with orange felt (see photograph on back cover). A ready-made writing-pad costs no more to buy than to make oneself. You have only to cover the four corners with orange felt, finished off at the back, to make it match the rest of the set.

To cover the blotter, release the curved metal plate, over which the blotting-paper is stretched, from the holder, pressing it gently against the holder and pushing it out, sideways or downwards according to the make. Then coat the empty holder all over with adhesive, with special attention to the under parts; and cover it with orange felt, cut rather larger, as in the case of the pen-tray, because the edges will be trimmed off when the whole is dry. Then replace the blotting-paper stretcher in the holder. When everything has been covered to match, make a flower in light-green felt with a black spot in the centre, for each article, and gum it into the top left-hand corner.

It's not difficult to cover useful objects with felt, always remembering not to cut the felt too small to begin with, and to press it flat, without blisters or wrinkles.

Table mats for children

Materials:

1 piece of medium-blue felt, 20 × 14 inches,

1 piece of red felt, 14 × 14 inches (or scraps of red felt).

Cut the shapes of a spoon, fork, tea-spoon, mug and plate out of the red felt, and glue them on the mat

at the places where the real objects will be, so that the child will learn their proper arrangement. The two narrow sides of the mat can be trimmed with pinking scissors, but in any case the trimming must be done without a stop, or the edge will look uneven (see picture: the left edge shows several stops, the right edge is straight.)

If the mat is intended for a quite small child, it is advisable to enclose it in a plastic bag the same size. This will keep it clean, and the child can still see the pattern through it. On Sundays and holidays the bag can be taken off as a treat, and then he will take special care of it (p. 15).

Simple table-mat with spoon and fork, etc. glued on. Instructions for making the 'rabbit' egg-cosy will be found on p. 20.

Hat box

Materials:
1 piece of pink felt, wide enough to go round the box and twice its height,
1 square piece of pink felt the width of the lid, 1 strip of light-green felt as wide as the rim of the lid and long enough to go round it,
2 squares of light-green felt, 6×6 inches,
2 squares of pink felt, 4×4 inches,
1 yard of silk ribbon, pink or green to match the felt.

You can get a hat-box at a hat shop or the millinery department of a store, or make one yourself. With a strip of cardboard the height of the box, form a cylinder by gluing the ends together. Cut a circular piece for the bottom and fasten the cylinder to it with a strip of material, gluing one half of the width of this to the cylinder, and the other to the bottom. To cover the box, coat the top and bottom edges with gelatinous adhesive, and vertically at two opposite places on the sides. Then lay the felt round the body of the box and press it on, beginning at one of the upright glued places and winding it slowly round until the cut edges meet without overlapping. The lower edge of this covering strip must exactly reach the bottom outside, and the top one, folded over the rim and gummed down to form the lining, must reach it inside. Although the inside area of the box is slightly smaller than the outside, the felt won't wrinkle; it can easily be slightly compressed as you flatten it. Glue one of the felt squares on the lid of the box and trim away the surplus material. Then glue the narrow strip of green felt round the outside of the rim, trimming the edge with the pinking scissors if you like. The inside of the lid is left unlined. Make two rosettes of different sizes out of the light-green felt squares and two out of the pink ones. Then glue them together in alternating colours, the larger ones under the smaller, and glue this decoration either in the middle or towards the side of the lid. Cut the green, or pink, silk ribbon in two equal lengths, and make two horizontal slits in opposite sides of the box between cardboard and lining, the width of the

ribbon, and pull one end of it through each slit, gluing it firmly between lining and cardboard. The box is now finished, and can be used not only for hats but for keeping scarves, caps, gloves and so forth.

Laundry bin

Materials:
Cardboard as for the hat-box,
but without the lid,
1 piece of light-green felt to go round the bin, and twice its height. 1 zipper, the length of the diameter of the bottom.

A waste-paper bin is easily obtainedt If you haven't one in the house, ge. one from a hardware store. The felt is glued on to it in the same way as with the hat-box, and it could then be used simply as a decorated waste-paper basket. But if you provide it with a loose bag you can have a handsome laundry bin, the purpose of which nobody can guess. The washing can be carried away in it just as it is.
The bag is made of a wide strip of felt, long enough to go round the bin. Sew the ends together (see sketch),

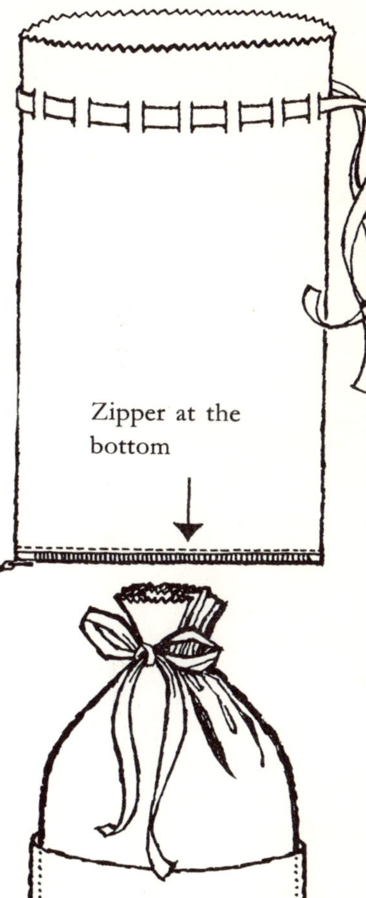

taking up just enough turnings to make the bag fit snugly into the bin. For easy emptying, sew a zipper into the bottom. Make slits, at equal distances apart, about 3 inches from the top, through which to thread the ribbon to close the bag. Then simply drop the bag into the bin: the felt is so firm that even when empty it won't collapse.

Hand-sewn work

Saucepan-lid holder

Materials:
1 piece of felt, 12 × 16 inches, scraps of felt of a contrasting colour, embroidery thread.

It may seem unpractical to make a saucepan-lid holder in the form of a felt glove, but don't worry, felt washes as well as any other material. First cut out a paper pattern, leaving plenty of room for your hand, besides ¼-inch all round for turnings. Don't make the thumb too wide, or you won't have a firm grasp. Cut the pattern double, so that you can glue the two sides together and try the glove on before cutting out the two felt pieces. Cut the fabric as continuously as you can, to keep the outline even. Before sewing the two sides together, cut a heart, or some other shape, out of felt of a different colour, and sew it on to the back of the glove. To give the work a nice touch, use embroidery thread of the same colour as the decoration for sewing the glove together in buttonhole stitch. The glove in the photograph is bright blue and dark red. As a finishing touch, make a loop to hang the glove up by out of a strip of felt sewn together at the edges.

This holder is an easy bit of needle-work for children. The heart on the back of the glove is optional: any other design would do.

Rabbit egg-cosy

Materials:
Small scraps of felt in different colours, including 2 pieces, 4×4 inches, of the same colour.

First cut out the basic form of the cosy (an equilateral triangle) twice. The sides must all measure 4 inches in length and be slightly curved (see sketch). Sew these triangles together with small buttonhole stitches, to form a bell, and oversew the bottom edge in buttonhole stitch to match. Then cut the rabbit's head and the upper part of its body out of felt of another colour (twice) and the ears out of another colour (not two pairs, because they are not made double), buttonholing the edges. Sew the two body-and-head pieces together with

The basic shape is an equilateral triangle. The drawings of body, head and ears are easily enlarged.

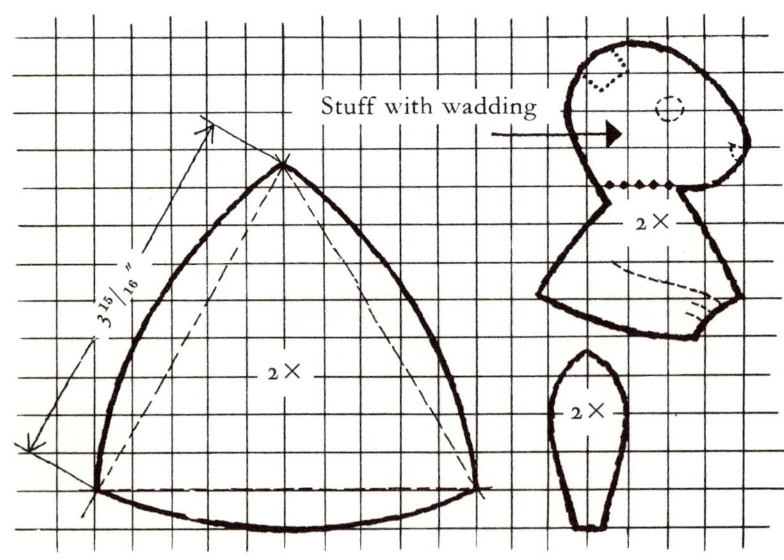

The rabbit egg-cosy is made on a simple basic pattern in three parts: body, head, with neck, and ears. Body and head can also be made out of the same piece.

buttonhole stitching, leaving the bottom edge open. Stuff the head with wadding, and then fit the body over the top of the cosy and sew it on firmly, taking care not to catch in the opposite side, or the cosy will become sewn together at the top. Last of all, sew on the ears, and embroider eyes, nose and paws (colour plate p. 14).

Calendar-holder
'Four Seasons'

Materials:
1 piece of felt, linen or woollen material, 8 × 20 inches, in dark green; felt scraps in brown, white, yellow, blue, black, violet, light-green and olive (or any other colours),
1 piece of lining material, 6 × 18 inches, in any colour preferred.

First measure off 1 inch all round the dark-green background strip, turn this to the back and press it. Divide the length of the remaining space (18 inches) into four equal sections and mark them with basting thread. Then cut your motifs out free-hand: bright-coloured flowers in simple shapes, conventionalized stems and leaves in light-green felt. For the summer, a yellow sun (using the foot of a liqueur-glass as a templet).
For autumn, a brown tree-trunk with olive-green or lightbrown leaves. For winter, a snowman (out of two round pieces) with a black top hat.
You can of course take other things as symbols of the seasons, such as a bird and its nest, a sailing-boat, a kite and a toboggan; but they must

The calendar-holder is a particularly pretty present, a practical wall decoration that will give pleasure for many a year.

always be simple, without superfluous detail, so that they can be easily recognised at a distance. Lay them on the foundation strip, and fix them temporarily with adhesive tape in case they need altering. When their positions are settled, hem them down neatly with small stitches. The flowers in the spring motif need only a stitch or two in the centre; they will look livelier if their edges are left loose. The tree-trunk and falling leaves, too, need only a row of stitches through the middle, so that their outlines stand away from the back. Do this in backstitching. Sewing on the motifs may appear a tedious job, but it takes surprisingly little time: one long evening is enough. When the work is finished it must be laid on something soft, and pressed from the back under a damp cloth. The appliqué work will be pushed into the soft underlay and remain unflattened. Remove the basting threads marking the spaces, beforehand.

Now glue a strip of cardboard about 2 inches wide across the whole width of the lining, using gelatinous adhesive. When the glue is dry, lay the lining on the foundation, with the cardboard against the wrong side of this, below the snowman, and between foundation and lining, to serve as a support for the calendar block. The lining must be exactly the width of the foundation. Pin it in position, and then sew the edges of the foundation to it with small, neat stitches. Finally, make two upright slits at the bottom of the holder to take the metal attachments of the calendar block, which must go through all three layers: foundation, cardboard and lining. If the foundation is not made of felt, the slits must be edged with buttonhole stitching.

To hang up the calendar-holder, sew two curtain rings to the top corners, or buy a hanging attachment at an ironmonger's or an embroidery shop (see photograph). These metal hangers with a ring and screws are used in Scandinavia, Holland and Switzerland for the bell-pulls in use there. They are not cheap, (colour photograph on the cover).

Measurement board for children

Materials:
2 pieces of olive-green felt, 12×60 inches,
1 piece of yellow felt or linen, 8×30 inches,
1 piece of dark lining material 19×58 inches,
felt scraps in brown, red, orange and light green,
yellow wool

The measurement board is made on the same principle as the calendar-holder (p. 22), all the decorations being sewn down on the foundation material. After sewing the lining to the back of the strip, mark off the inch-divisions on the right or left edge of the front at every two inches, numbering every fourth. Make the marks first with tailor's chalk, and then with small back-stitches in yellow wool. You can make a little doll out of the yellow wool, to hang on a long string and be placed at the child's height. If there are several children, make little dolls of different colours, so that every child has its own colour.

This wall-hanging is for children to measure their height by. It must be hung so that the first mark is exactly 44 inches from the floor. The decorations are sewn on, and the figures embroidered. Of course the strip can be made longer, and begin at 20 inches. Then the giraffe will have a body and legs.

Jobs for the sewing-machine

(can also be carried out by hand)

Lion - for riding and snoozing on

Materials:
1 piece of yellow felt, 18 × 38 inches,
2 yellow felt squares, 13 × 13 inches,
1 strip of brown felt, 6 × 38 inches
(possibly joining several strips together),
felt scraps in brown and orange for the face,
thick black wool-yarn for the tail,
foam rubber flakes for the stuffing.

The lion takes the form of a big pillow, and is very easy to make. Its head and rump consist of 2 large round pieces of felt, 12 inches in diameter, which can be cut out round a long-playing record. The centre of one of these rounds must be marked through the hole in the centre of the record, and a cross-shaped cut made there to take the tail—a braid of thick black wool yarn, bound at each end. Push one end of the tail through the slit and sew it on all round on the inside with heavy thread (twine or button thread). For greater security you can glue a small circle of cardboard behind the opening in the felt, push the tail through this and tie it in a stout knot. Then sew the felt firmly to the tail on the outside.

Now cut eyes, nose and mouth out of bits of brown felt and sew them down neatly on the other round of felt. For the cheeks, cut 2 rounds of orange felt, using the foot of a wine-glass as a templet, and sew them on. You can omit them, but the lion will look much less friendly.

When you cut out the two large circles from the felt squares, eight corners were left over, and four of

these can now be used for the ears. Cut them to your taste, in two matching pairs, and sew them double, with the stitching outside.

The big piece of felt for the body can now be sewn up on the long sides to form a cylinder, leaving about 6 inches open in the middle of the

Children like playing with the simplest of soft animal toys, made to stand up to the most temperamental cuddlings without harm. The lion can be washed or cleaned.

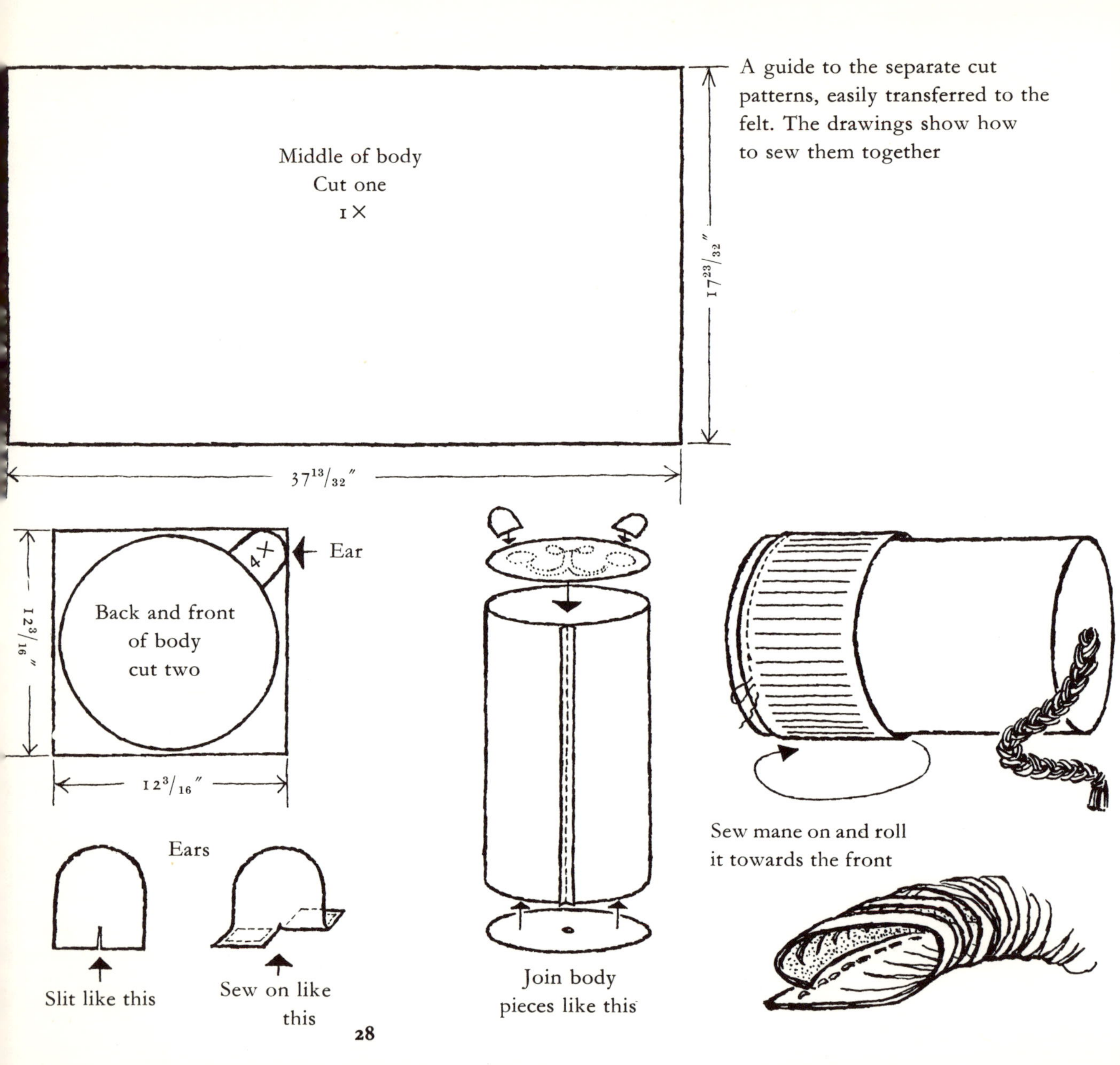

Middle of body
Cut one
1 ✕

A guide to the separate cut
patterns, easily transferred to the
felt. The drawings show how
to sew them together

17 23/32 "

37 13/32 "

Ear
4 +

Back and front
of body
cut two

12 3/16 "

12 3/16 "

Ears

Slit like this

Sew on like
this

Join body
pieces like this

Sew mane on and roll
it towards the front

seam for stuffing the body. Then sew in the two circles, right sides towards the inside of the cylinder, first basting them in place in case adjustments are needed to its width. If you have kept carefully to the measurements, however, keeping the seams the right width, everything should fit. Sew the head to the body so that the seam in the latter is underneath, i.e. with the mouth exactly above the seam. It doesn't matter how you sew on the rump, as the tail will fall in any direction. When you have got this far, turn the work right side out, and fill the body with foam rubber flakes (obtainable from bedding stores, upholsterers, saddlers, etc.) It will take a lot: you will need about two bags the size of the body—but fortunately, it is cheap. When the stuffing is finished, close the seam. Now comes the mane. Fold the strip of brown felt in two, lengthways, and make slits in it at intervals of $\frac{3}{8}$-inch, leaving $\frac{3}{4}$-inch uncut at the edges; the slits will then be $4\frac{1}{2}$ inches long when you unfold the strip again. First sew one edge of this 'mane' to the seam between body and head, by hand; then lay the other edge over the first and sew it down in the same way, so that the mane becomes a series of loops. Finally, sew on the ears, right and left, behind the mane. To make them stand up, make a $\frac{3}{8}$-inch slit at the middle of the lower edge and sew one half of the ear towards the back and the other towards the front (photograph on cover).

When making this cuddly animal, be careful to sew everything very firmly; children are notoriously careless in the treatment of their possessions.

Tea-cosy and egg-cosies

Materials (for the tea-cosy):
2 pieces of pink felt, 10 × 12 inches,
1 piece of violet felt, 1 yd long by
2¾ inches wide (join shorter strips if
necessary),
cotton material for lining (the size of
the felt),
foam rubber or wadding as interlay,
knitting wool in light-green and
olive-green.

To make the cosy, first cut out the
front and back pieces. To shape them,
use a long-playing record for round-
ing the top. Lay one piece of felt on
the table with the narrow sides horizontal, then lay the record on it,
touching the middle at the top, and
draw round it with a pencil as far as
the sides. Cut the other piece of felt to
match, then cut off as much of the
violet strip as will reach right round
the cosy from one bottom corner to
the other, measuring it carefully
along the edge and allowing ½-inch
over.
The strip can be made in several
pieces. The front of the cosy can be
either embroidered, or decorated, like
the model, with a crochet rosette.
This rosette, made on an old Danish
pattern, is in two colours—light-
green and olive-green, worked with a
No. 4 hook as follows: Make three
chain stitches in dark wool-yarn and
join them. 1st round: 10 plain
crochet. 2nd round: 1 long treble,
1 chain, alternately. Into every third
plain stitch of the last round make 2
long trebles. 3rd round: ¾ make scallops with 4 chain and 1 plain. 4th
round: with light wool work five
chain and one picot out of 5 chain.

5th round: with dark wool make scallops of 6 chain, (or more or fewer stitches to equalize the pattern). After every scallop, make a plain stitch into the picot of the last round. Press the finished rosette under a damp cloth and sew it on to the felt with small stitches. By way of finish, embroider rays, starting from a scallop between the light-coloured picots and reaching over the edge of the rosette. Tack the violet strip round the edge of the embroidered piece (which must face inwards) from one bottom corner to the other, leaving the ends free. Sew it on, by hand or machine, and then baste and sew it to the other piece in the same way. Turn the work right side out and press it under a damp cloth like an ordinary woollen material, taking care not to stretch it. Make a stitched loop out of a scrap of the pink felt for

The tea- and egg-cosies shown here were made as a set, in felt of strongly contrasted colours.

The rosette on the tea-cosy was crocheted after a Danish pattern (see cover).

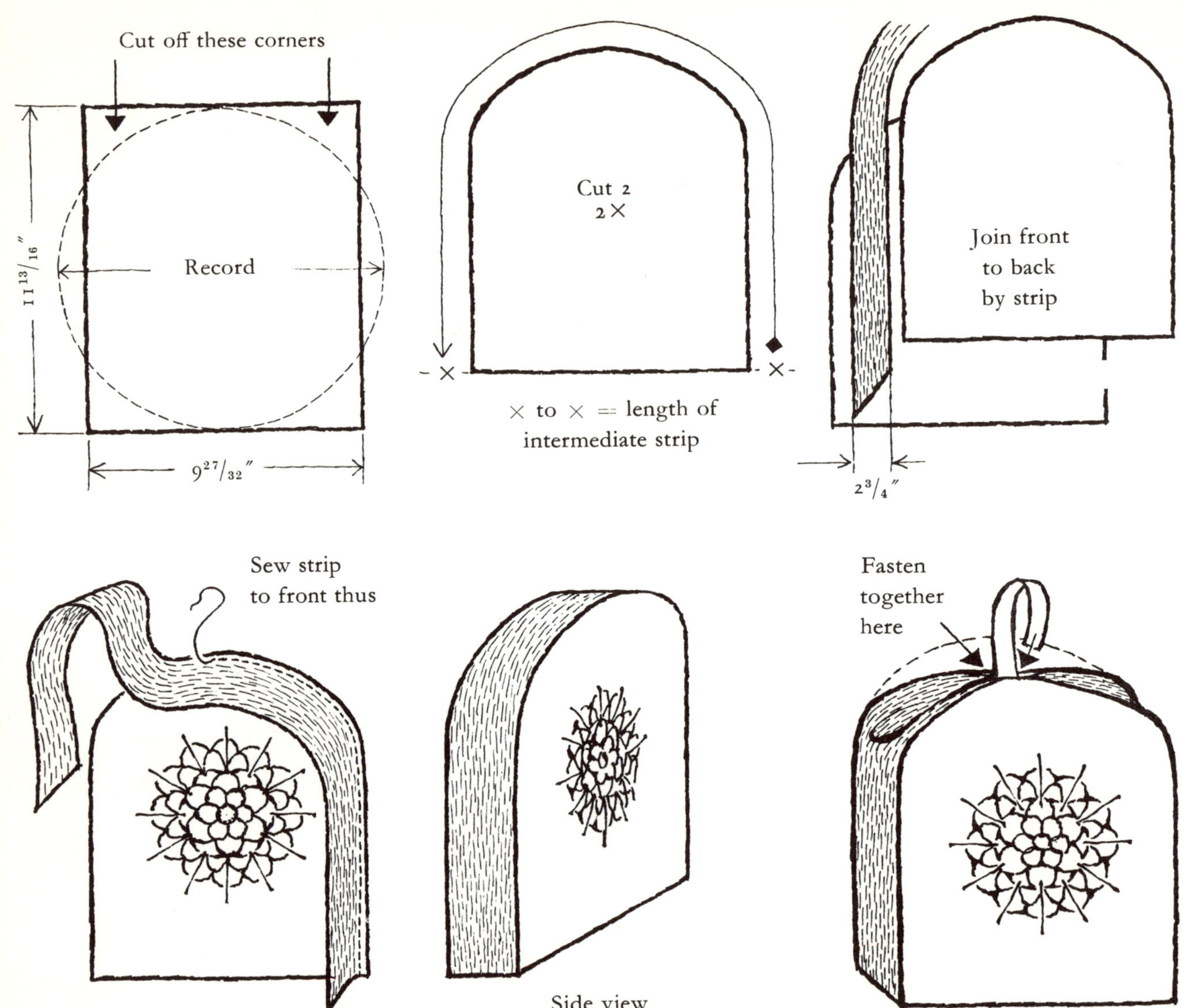

Cut off these corners
11 13/16 "
Record
9 27/32 "
Cut 2
2 ×
× to × = length of
intermediate strip
Join front
to back
by strip
2 3/4 "
Sew strip
to front thus
Side view
Fasten
together
here

The drawings show the separate
parts and working stages.
Padding and lining are cut on
the same pattern, slightly smaller.

removing the cosy or hanging it up.
Set this in between the two pink
sides, pushing the violet strip inwards and pulling the top of the cosy
together, securing it firmly with
invisible stitches. This finishes the
cover.

Now comes the padding. Cut the
lining out of cotton stuff the same
colour as the felt and join it in the
same way. The interlining of wadding
or foam rubber must be $1\frac{1}{2}$ inches
shorter at the bottom and $\frac{1}{4}$-inch
smaller round the other edges. Baste
it to the wrong side of the lining with
big zigzag stitches, and then turn the
lower edge of the lining over the edge
of the wadding and baste it firmly.
Lastly, pull the felt cover over the
lining and interlining, turning it in at
the bottom and sewing it neatly to
the lining. The egg-cosies are made
in the same way, out of two $3\frac{1}{2}$-inch

squares and an intermediate strip
$1\frac{1}{4} \times 8\frac{1}{4}$ inches. Instead of the crochet
work, decorate them with an em-
broidered rosette in two colours
(colour photograph on cover).

Violet cushion cover

Materials:
2 pieces of violet felt, 14×14 inches,
1 piece of orange felt, 10×10 inches,
violet sewing cotton.

Cut eight leaves out of the orange felt,
all differing a little in shape, and sew
them neatly on to one of the violet
pieces in the form of a conventionalized flower. Then embroider free-

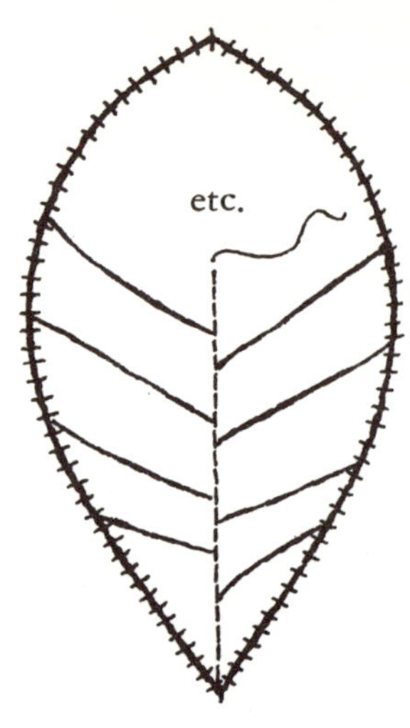

You could make the leaves a different shape altogether, or instead of leaves cut out geometrical shapes (circles, diamonds or squares) and use them in the same way. When the embroidery is done, sew the two halves of the cushion cover together on the wrong side on three sides, turn it right side out and close the fourth side after inserting the cushion. You could, of course, close it with a zipper, but it would be difficult to find one in such a vivid colour. Other colour schemes could include light-/dark-green, light-/dark-blue, red/pink, olive-green/brown, dark-green/dark-red (see back cover).

You can make a lot of things in in felt and try them out on a cushion. Here orange leaves were sewn on a violet ground and partly embroidered.

hand some fine ribs and veins on four of the leaves (or on all eight if you like—but it will look more interesting if you do it in the order seen in the photograph).

Green cushion cover

Materials:
2 pieces of light-green felt, 14 × 14 inches,
1 piece of batiste or similar material, 4 × 4 inches.

Lay the felt on the cushion and mark the best position for the monogram, allotting a square of about 3 × 3 inches to this. Then draw the monogram carefully in block capitals on the felt with a soft pencil, taking care to have as few intersections as possible. The letters can also be placed below or beside one another. Wrong lines can be erased with a soft indiarubber eraser, but avoid distorting the felt in doing this, or stretching it too hard, or it will get blisters, which will have to be ironed out under a damp cloth. When the monogram is ready, baste the square of batiste under it on the inside of the felt, and machinestitch the outlines of the letters, or backstitch them by hand. Where they intersect, only the stitching of one initial must go right through, i.e. that of the surname, and the lines crossing these must be interrupted there, and started again further on (see the curve

Monograms on felt can be embroidered; they can consist of letters cut out and applied, or, as here, have an underlay of batiste and be stitched round.

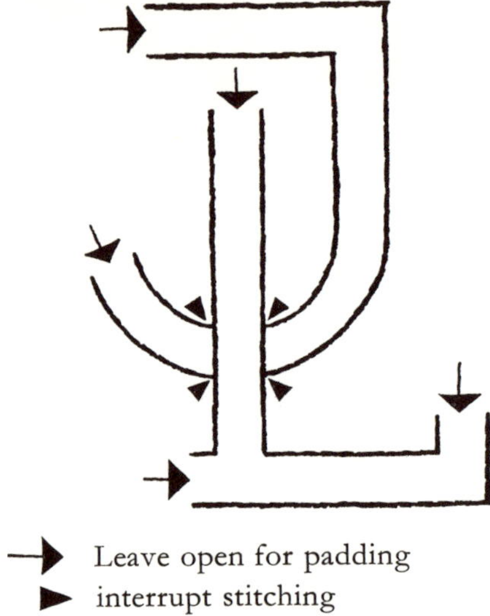

pieces from the back on three sides, turn the work right side out and slip it over the cushion. Close the opening by hand with invisible stitches (see back cover).

Orange cushion cover

Materials:
2 pieces of orange felt, 14×14 inches,
1 piece of violet felt, 10×10 inches,
orange silk thread.

of the J in drawing and photograph). The ends of the initials are left unsewn because they must remain open for little rolls of wadding to be pushed into them from the back, between batiste and felt, after you have removed the basting threads. The narrower the letters, the more difficult it is to pad them. Try pushing the wadding in with a matchstick or the end of a crochet-hook. Finish off the open ends by hand with small back stitches and secure the ends of all the loose threads.

Now you have only to join the two

Cut four identical leaf shapes out of the violet felt, about $4\frac{1}{2}$ inches long and $3\frac{1}{4}$ inches across the widest part. Mark the centre of one of the halves of the cover, and place the ends of the leaves $\frac{1}{2}$-inch away from this, lying in four directions. Sew them on with small but visible stitches in orange silk, and before completing the outline push a little wadding under them, to make them stand out from the background. Then complete the stitching.

All four leaves are sewn on like this and lightly padded. Do this evenly, or

The four leaves on this cushion were sewn on to an orange ground with small stitching, over an underlay of wadding. Other motifs can, of course, be used in the same way.

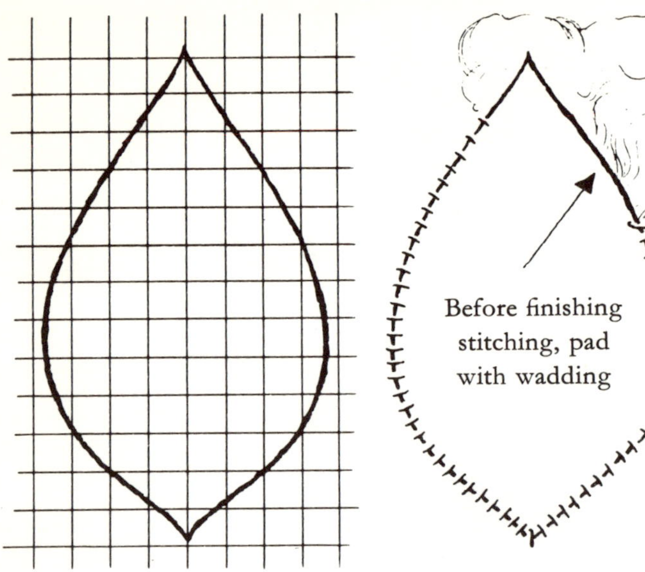

String bag

Materials:
1 piece of olive-green felt, 8 × 20 inches (or 2 pieces 8 × 12 inches), felt scraps for appliqués.

Safe in this handsome bag, which can serve as a wall hanging, the string is convenient and free of tangles. The bag illustrated is olive-green, the flower orange, stalk and leaves yellow. All these can be drawn freehand on the bits of felt, and cut out. Cut a hole in the middle of the flower. Machinestitch flower and stalk to the front of the bag. Do not sew the leaves down at the edges but only in the middle, to give them a more plastic effect. Make an opening for the string in the middle of the

The drawing above shows the shape of a leaf (optional); that on the right, the wadding being pushed in.

some will show up more than the others, giving the work a distorted appearance. Now lay the two halves of the cover together, right sides facing, stitch them together on three sides, turn the work and slip it over the cushion. Close the opening by hand (back cover).

The string bag opposite can be made of two pieces of felt or a single one. The two-piece one is seamed at the bottom.

Cut hole for string like this

flower, right through the bag itself, by cutting radiating slits. Fold the material in half, right side outwards, then fold to form the bottom of the bag, and sew up the sides, allowing the stitches to show. If the bag is made in two pieces, these must, of course, be joined at the bottom as well. Finally, make vertical slits about ½ inch long and 1 inch apart, 3 inches below the top of the bag, to take a cord of twisted or crocheted string.

A bag of this kind can be used for knitting yarn, too, or you can keep string of two different thicknesses in it by sewing it together down the middle to make two separate pockets. In that case you must apply two separate, smaller motifs and make a hole in each.

'Kangaroo' laundry-bag

Materials:
2 pieces of grey-beige felt, 20 × 30 inches,
1 piece of light-green felt, 16 × 16 inches,
1 piece of tape, 14 inches long, in grey-beige or light-green,
felt scraps in red, black and orange,
3 white buttons.

First make a paper pattern of the kangaroo, beginning at the bottom with part of a circle, then running the side lines towards each other in the shape of a big pear.
You can easily draw a head in profile at the top. This done, fold the drawing lengthways down the middle and cut the pattern out of the doubled paper as far as the neck, so that the two sides are alike, correcting the lines if necessary as you go. The patterns for ears and legs are cut separately. Fit all the pieces together to see if the proportions are about right, and then cut them out in the felt. The material must not be laid double when cutting out, or the edges, which show on the outside, won't be neat. All the parts—two

bodies, two ears and four legs—must be cut separately out of the beige felt, and two ears out of the light-green (for the inside). Cut a light-green waistcoat for the kangaroo, first making a paper pattern for it.

Now for the sewing. First cut a curved slit in the front of the body, 12 inches wide and 10 inches at its lowest point from the bottom of the body (see drawing). This will form the pocket-hole. Back the lower edge of the slit with a piece of tape and stitch them together near the edge. Sew down the waistcoat at the neck opening and across the body, but not at the sides.

Stitch a line down the middle of the waistcoat to suggest the opening, and sew the three buttons on it. Add an orange tie at the neckline. Stitch the four leg pieces together in pairs, close to the edges, and attach them to the waistcoat as in the picture. The details for the face can be cut out and

It's quite easy to make a kangaroo without a special pattern, if you start from very simple basic forms, as in this drawing.

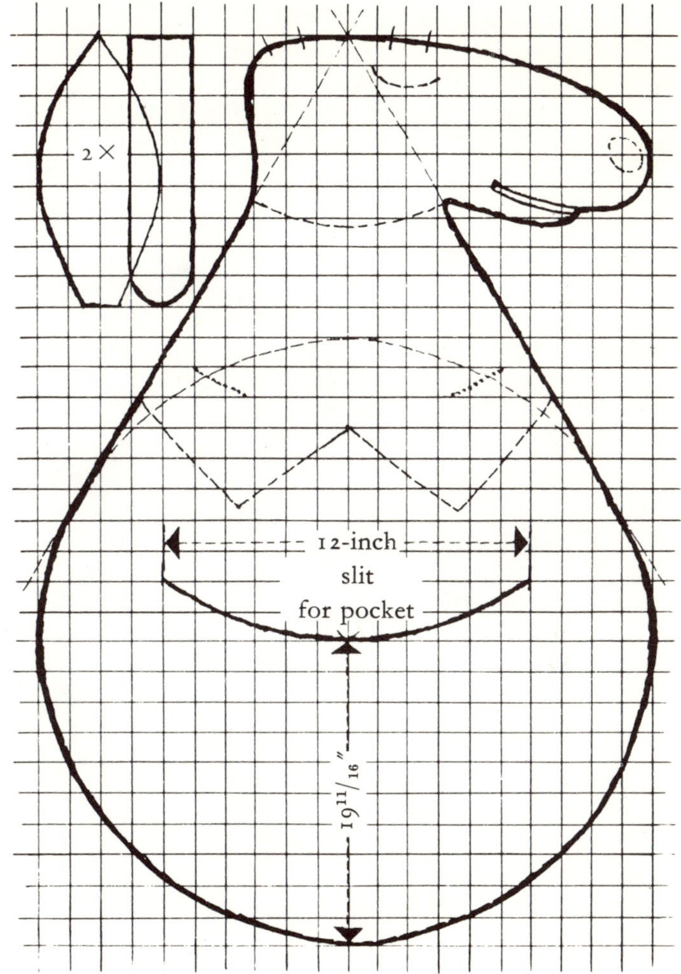

sewn on now, or left till the end. Stitch the ear-pieces together—inside beige and outside green—and slip them between back and front before tacking these together. Where the waistcoat has to be included there will be a triple thickness to sew. When everything fits properly (perhaps after making a few slight corrections with the scissors, taking care not to stretch the fabric), sew the two sides together near the edge with small stitches. The upper edge of the pocket-hole must be sewn to the back half of the body. To hang the bag up, sew a curtain ring behind each ear.

The kangaroo makes a nice wall hanging for the nursery, apart from its purpose in keeping things tidy. It holds the children's dirty clothes in its pocket—and no doubt many a surprise as well.

Needlework case ('Housewife')

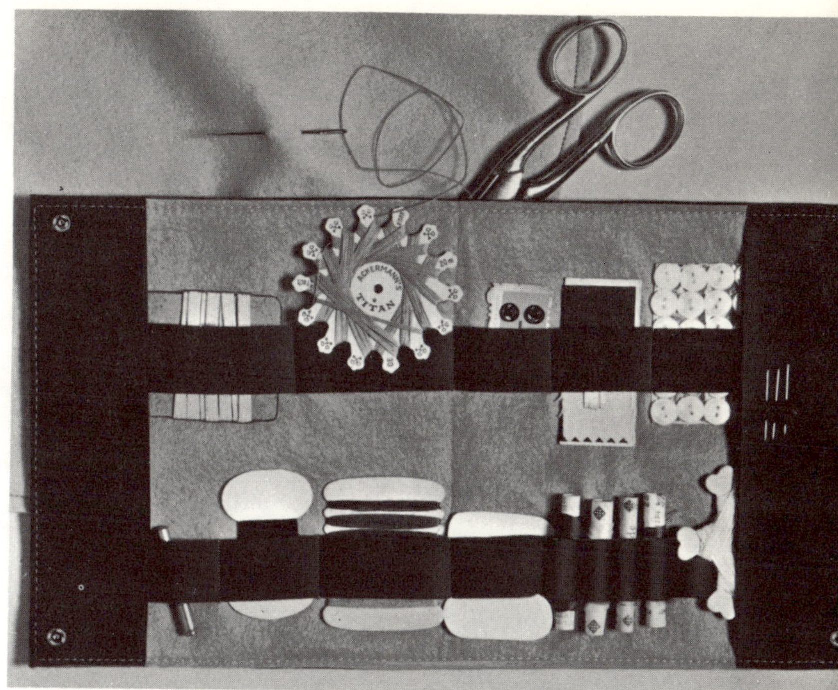

Materials:
1 piece of dark-blue felt, 8 × 16 inches,
1 piece of light-blue felt, 8 × 12 inches.

Cut two inch-wide strips from the long side of the dark-blue felt, lay them on the light-blue felt and pin them to it at intervals, to form loops for taking thread, needles, buttons, elastic and other sewing requisites, settling the size of the loops by trying them over the objects themselves. Take care, when doing this, not to let the light-blue ground pucker; if it does, the loops will be too small for their purpose and you will have to allow more play. As the photograph shows, the strips run horizontally over the whole width of the foundation (12 inches), but as they are 16 inches long, once the loops have been allowed for, some of the ends may have to be cut away, and the strips sewn down as prepared. The ends of the threads must be firmly fastened off at the back, or the loops will work loose again. Now sew the light felt ground on to the dark blue, leaving 2 inches of this on either side, to be turned back over the light ground and stitched to it at the top and bottom of the ends. Lastly, close the case like a book and sew press-buttons on both corners.

A flat needlework case is both pretty and useful. It will come in handy not only in the suitcase but in the writing-table drawer.

The little needlework case is
fastened with two press-buttons
at the corners. It is dark-blue
on the outside and light-blue
inside.

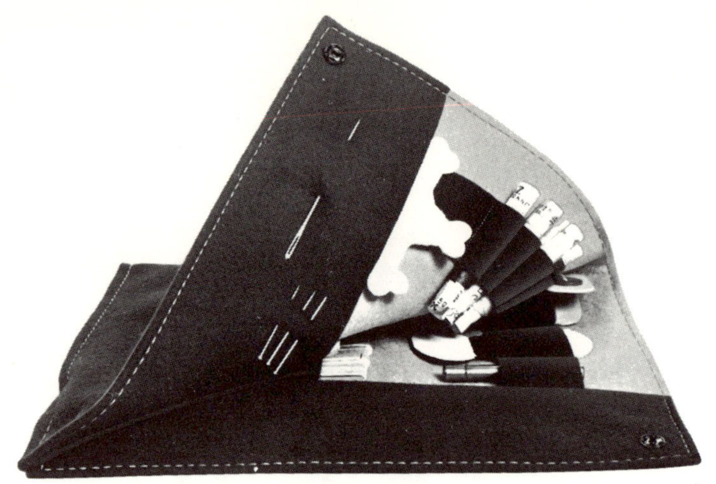

Travelling shoe-bag with trees

Materials:
2 pieces of felt of any colour, 13×18
inches,
2 pieces of felt, 4×4 inches, the same
colour, foam rubber flakes.

Cut a strip $1\frac{1}{2}$ inches wide off each
of the two large pieces before sewing
them together on three sides, a little
way in from the edges, to form a bag.
The top of the bag can either be
finished with overcast stitching, or
cut with pinking scissors, and the

seams are shown on the outside. Mark the middle of the bag on the bottom seam, and stitch it together towards the top for about 12 inches, to divide the bag into two compartments — one for each shoe. With the strips cut off at the beginning make a tie for the bag by first joining them and then folding them lengthways in three, first from left to right and then the reverse way, $\frac{1}{2}$ inch each time.

Machine-stitch these three layers together down one side. Cut two pieces 4 inches long off this tie, and sew the remainder to one side of the bag, 4 inches from the upper edge, keeping the ends more or less equal. The two 4 × 4 inch pieces of felt are for making the shoetrees. Use the top half of an insole the right size as a pattern, allowing $\frac{3}{4}$ inch extra all round. Cut four pieces from this

Shoe-bag and trees in light-blue felt. Useful not only for travelling but when going to the theatre or to a ball.

pattern and stitch them together in pairs, leaving the edges and seams to show on the outside. Leave a space open opposite the toe, through which to stuff the little bags very tight with foam rubber flakes. Stuffing them with wadding wouldn't be much use, because after a time it would become lumpy and give no support to the shoe. Before closing the seam insert a little loop in each tree and sew it fast. These loops are made of the cuttings from the long tie. To ensure that the trees always keep the same side towards the sole of the shoe and take on a shape of their own in time, sew little marks on the upper side. These can be made of felt, or of woollen lace, as in the picture. The ends of the tie can also be decorated.

The shoe-bag will be useful not only for travelling, but for shoes to change into at the theatre, where it can be given to the cloakroom attendant with your street shoes.

Dolls: 'Romeo and Juliet'

Materials:
2 pieces of yellow felt, 16×18 inches (for one doll),
large and small scraps for clothes,
hair and face,
foam rubber flock

'Romeo' and 'Juliet' are the names of these two comical creatures, made entirely of felt. Their bodies are stuffed with foam rubber flock, so that they can be washed.

Both dolls are made on the same basic pattern. Only their stride is different, and, of course, their hair-do.

Juliet

Romeo

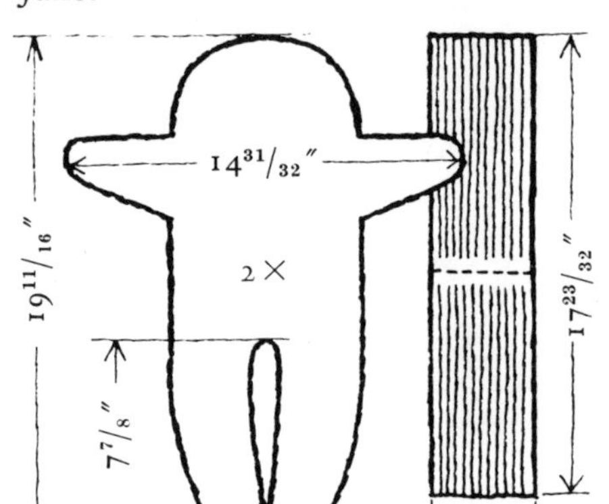

The cut-out pattern is practically the same for both dolls, only 'Romeo' has shorter legs because the slit between them ends lower down. Cut two pieces (back and front) of the same shape, for each doll, and sew them together with reasonable turnings, leaving a 4-inch opening at one side for turning right side out and stuffing. Where corners occur in the sewing (between the legs, at the armholes and the neck), slit the edges about ⅛ inch to prevent the stuff from pulling. After turning them right side out, stuff first the arms and legs, and then the body and head, with foam rubber flock, before sewing up the opening by hand. The faces can be made as you like. Eyes and mouth, even a nose, can be glued on, unless the doll is to be given to a very small child, when it is safer to sew them on, or even embroider them. Even the dolls' hair is made of felt. Romeo's two-tier crew-cut is sewn along the head seam, to fall forward. Juliet's mane is made of a cutting of felt $3\frac{1}{2} \times 12$ inches, cut into strips lengthways as far as the middle, which forms the parting and is sewn to the crown of the doll's head, from front to back, The strips are tied together on each side, like pigtails.

The dolls' clothes should be kept simple, without any trimming. Make them of felt, and use the drawings as basic patterns.

Using up felt scraps

Decorative covers for matchboxes

Materials:
2 pieces of unbleached linen $\frac{1}{4}$ inch wider and longer than the box,
scraps of coloured felt,
2 pieces of cardboard the size of the existing cover

Lay one of the pieces of cardboard on a piece of linen so that the material extends half an inch beyond it all round. Turn this surround over the cardboard and glue it down. Then coat the whole of that surface thinly with glue as well as the bottom of the matchbox cover. When the glue has become tacky, press the two surfaces together. Now take the other piece of linen and mark the outline of the other piece of cardboard on it with a soft pencil, leaving a half-inch

surround as before, and compose your appliqué design inside the pencil lines. Although appliqué motifs are usually sewn down flat on the background, here they should only be attached here and there, to give a livelier effect. If you want to copy the illustration, begin by weaving some narrow felt strips to form an area of about $2 \times 2\frac{1}{2}$ inches, after the fashion of the book-cover and marker (p. 9). Turn the edges of this under, to the shape of a basket and sew it on the linen with invisible stitches. This is a tricky job, but there isn't much of it, so don't lose patience! Now cut out flowers and leaves of every shape and colour from the felt scraps (see the suggestions on p. 50)
The flowers must only occasionally be sewn on to the linen through the centre, stalks and leaves at the bottom, or if necessary, again in the

Suggestions for making flowers
and leaves, with which to decorate
small surfaces

middle or at the top. All the stalks
and leaves must end at the rim of the
basket. They can cross, and conceal,
one another here and there, to make
the effect livelier. You can embroider
additional buds, stems and tendrils
directly on the linen. There is no end
to the possibilities, in fact, and you
should not be too conventional or
unimaginative. When the decoration
is finished, wrap the linen round the
cardboard as before, and glue down
the edges; then glue it to the front
of the matchbox cover.

If the friction strips on the sides of
the cover become worn out, strips
from a new box can be glued over
them.

A cheap, but not cheap-looking
present: a decorative case for a
large matchbox. Materials:
unbleached linen and a lot of
bright scraps of felt.

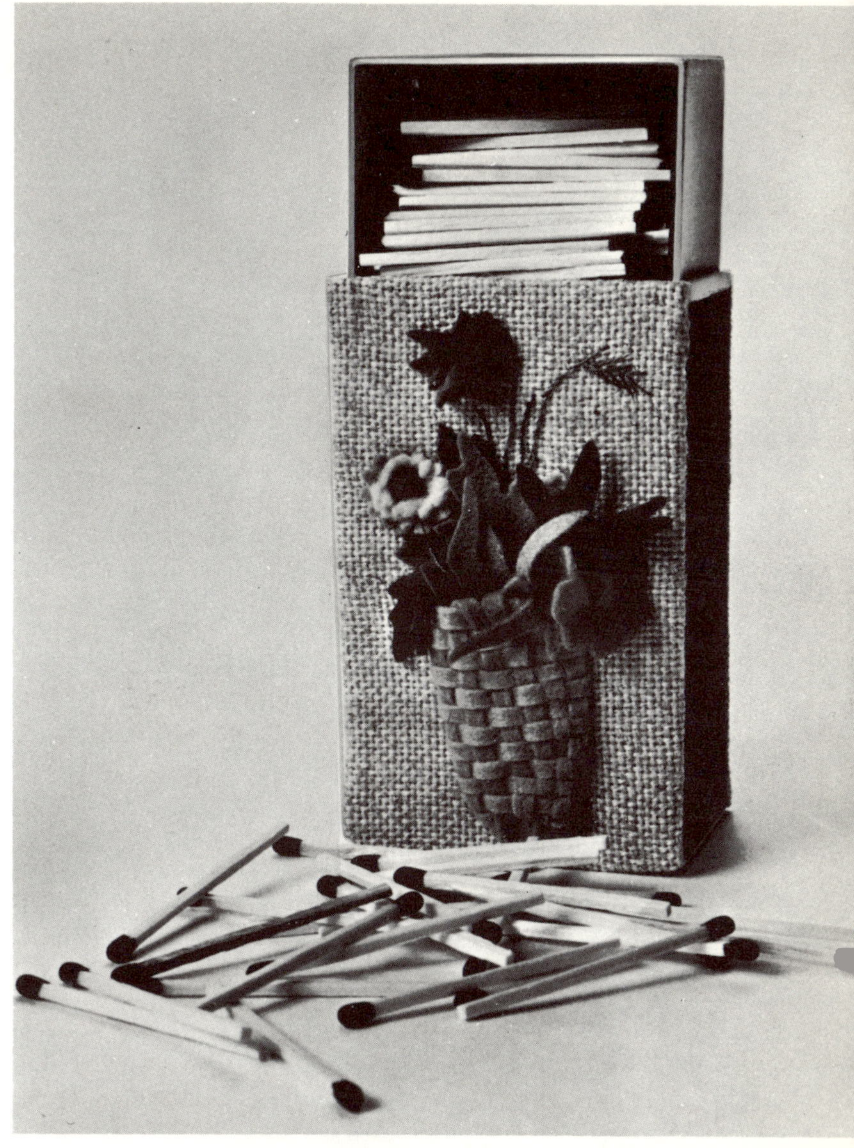

This is a key-bag for a child. If you insert a zipper in the slit it can be used as a purse.

'Eskimo' Key-bag

Materials:
1 piece of light-brown felt, 4×4 inches,
oddments of felt and embroidery thread in orange and green,
scraps of fur or teddy-bear material.

Cut the figure of the little Eskimo out of the square of brown felt, head and legs included, having first made a paper pattern for it. Then cut the little jacket out of orange felt, and give it a rich trimming of coloured felt strips and decorative stitching. The edges of the jacket must exactly cover those of the figure, to which it must be sewn at the neck, shoulders, sides and hem. Trim the ends of the jacket sleeves with a strip of felt sewn on with chainstitching, and trim the legs with chain-stitching in orange and green, to make them look as though he were wearing boots. Embroider the face, sewing on round cheeks cut out of felt. A ring of fur, cut to fit the head, will suggest the edges of a cap and make a frame to the face. It must be hemmed on.
Now cut a slit in the back, $\frac{1}{2}$ inch above the hem, and sew a piece of

Coat-hanger cover
with scent sachet

Materials:
2 strips of light-blue felt $\frac{3}{4}$ inch longer and wider than the hanger,
2 pieces of light-blue felt, $3\frac{1}{2} \times 4\frac{1}{2}$ inches,
scraps of coloured felt.

First unscrew the hook from the hanger; then cut two strips of felt exactly $\frac{3}{4}$ inch wider and longer than the hanger. The ends must fit those of the hanger, but there is no need to copy its slight curve. You can obtain this when sewing the two strips together (close to the edges) by stretching one of the seams a little and easing the other. Leave one end of the cover open till you have inserted the hanger, then close it with neat stitches. The cover must fit the hanger closely. If it is too loose, turn it inside out, so that the turnings are inside and take up the extra room. Before screwing the hook in again, coat it with a gelatinous adhesive and wind a narrow strip of felt or a bit of ribbon of the same colour. The sachet can be filled with woodruff or some other moth-preventive, or

black elastic inside at the neck seam, with a key ring on it. No child will lose its key so easily if it has such a pretty case. Given a zipper, it can also be used as a purse.

Pretty and practical: a dress-hanger covered in felt and a matching scent sachet. The sachet should only be lightly tied, so that you can really smell it.

with dried lavender blossoms or scented cottonwool. To make it, sew two pieces of felt, $3\frac{1}{2}\times 4$ inches, together on three sides, turning the upper edge in and hemming it. Make a felt tie out of a strip sewn double, and run this through the hem for attaching it to the dress-hanger. The front of the sachet can be decorated with little flowers in coloured felt (p. 50). It should only be loosely tied.

Baby's shoes with felt soles

Materials:
An old felt hat,
1 oz. of wool,
4 No. 10 or 11 needles.

An old felt hat can provide very good soles for a baby's crawling shoes. Make your pattern from an existing pair or by drawing round the child's foot, keeping the front of the soles wide enough not to cramp the toes. After cutting out the soles, iron them flat under a damp cloth. They can then be sewn to the soles of a pair of socks or woollen bootees. Or you can knit a pair of uppers for them. For a child of 14 to 18 months, proceed as follows:
Cast on 32 stitches and knit six rounds of alternate plain and purl. Then make a row of holes to take a twisted cord (knit 2 plain, wool forward, knit 2 together). Then knit another six rounds as before. For the instep slip 12 stitches on to one needle and work another 15 rows 1 purl, 1 plain, leaving the other 20 stitches for the heel. Then pick up the edge stitches on both sides of the instep to connect with the heel stitches again. Work three rounds purl, 3 rounds plain, and finally 4 rounds purl. Cast off, and sew the uppers to the soles with running stitches.

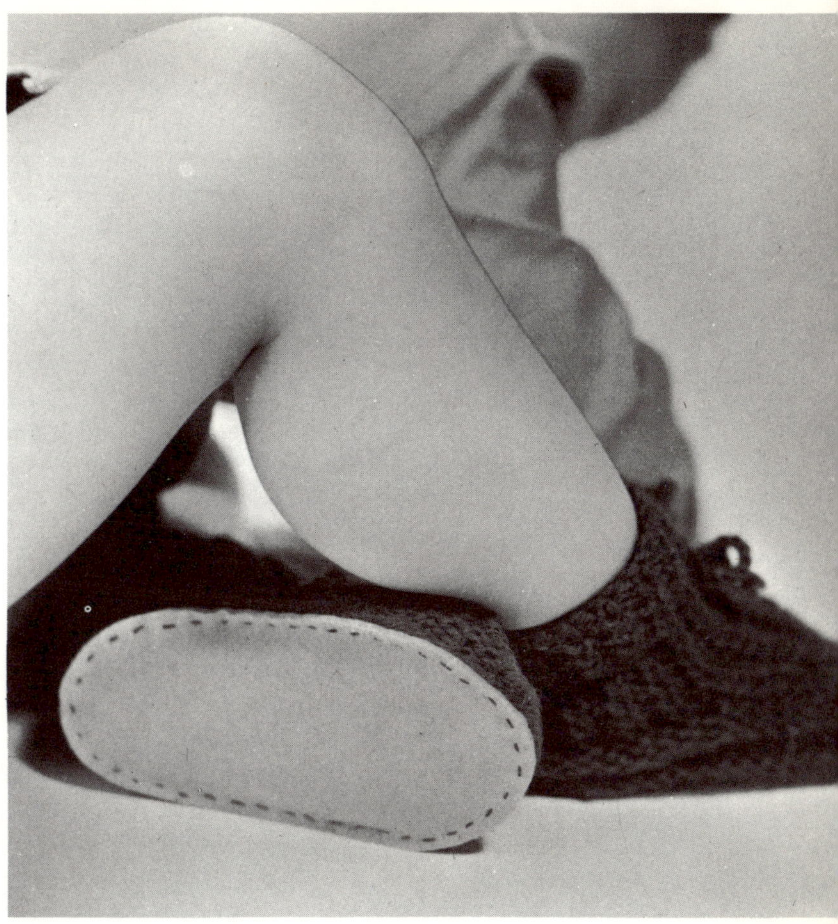

Soles for a child's house shoes can be cut from an old hat, or scraps of felt, and sewn to a pair of socks or home-knitted uppers.

Large wall hangings

Materials:
Union linen, coarse linen, strong cotton material or felt for the ground, felt in various colours and quantities according to the pattern,
adhesive iron-on material.

No exact list of materials can be given for wall hangings; the amounts needed depend on the size of the work on the one hand, and on the composition on the other. And as the cutting-out patterns could only be shown very reduced in size we haven't attempted to illustrate them.

A wall hanging like the one with the fishes (back cover) or the one on the opposite page showing a woman with the symbols of love and fertility, are jobs for experts. You can, of course, take your motifs from old pictures and patterns, but you should go your own way in carrying them out, so as to develop the creative capacity which alone gives a meaning to the hobby. Always bear simplicity in mind and never forsake the clear line for a fanciful one, which would be out of character. The best way to arrive at artistic and craftsmanlike results is by experimenting with gummed paper. Cut the motifs out of coloured paper and stick them on a paper ground the colour of the foundation, to test effect and harmony, adding or leaving out this or that. When composing, you can choose one of two ways: starting from the felt scraps at hand, or building up the design according to the pattern and procuring the material afterwards. Both methods are attractive, and can produce equally artistic results.

On the craft side, remember that in the case of large hangings the felt motifs should always be ironed on to adhesive material, because of the danger that the background material may stretch, owing to its weight, as soon as it is hung up, and if the felt pieces have been sewn on without a supporting underlay they will get stretched too, and will then unavoidably become distorted and appear crooked. But if you have ironed the felt on to some adhesive material before cutting it out, there will be no risk of this, and the whole hanging will acquire greater firmness. The motifs should be sewn on by hand, either with small hemming stitches, or in buttonhole stitching. Buttonhole stitching is more usual, and almost

classical, but the appliqué work of the
French art embroiderers is almost
exclusively carried out in hemming
stitch. The question whether each
motif should be sewn on with
matching thread, or whether they
should all be sewn with one colour
throughout, depends on the motif. If
it is a lively one it is better not to use
contrasting thread, or the effect will
be restless. But on large flat areas
everything can be sewn with the
same thread preferably the colour of
the foundation material.

A wall hanging like this is no job for a beginner; it is only suitable for somebody with a good deal of experience in shaping and working in felt.

Fun with Felt

Published 1969 by Watson-Guptill Publications,
a division of Billboard Publications, Inc.
165 W. 46 St., New York, New York
SBN 8230 1975 6

Library of Congress Catalog Card Number   Number 76-118115

Made and printed in the Netherlands
by the Ysel Press, Deventer